Vineg

Over 150
vinegar for cooking, [illegible] health

Compiled by Hugh Morrison

Montpelier Publishing
London
2015

ISBN-13: 978-1512136623
ISBN-10: 151213662X
Published by Montpelier Publishing, London.
Printed by Amazon Createspace.

.

Introduction

Everybody is familiar with the nursery rhyme about Jack and Jill going up the hill to fetch a pail of water, which ends with Jack tumbling down, breaking his crown, and Jill coming tumbling after.

Nowadays Jack and Jill would probably be rushed to hospital in an ambulance, but in the far off days of nursery rhymes, Jack had to make do with a homemade remedy. The final line of the rhyme says that Jack 'went to bed and bound his head/With vinegar and brown paper.'

If like me you've wondered why on earth he did this, then read on!

For vinegar is not just something to be sprinkled on chips. As Jack well knew, it reduces swellings and works as an antiseptic, and has many other medicinal uses. It's an effective cleaner which makes light work of all sorts of difficult jobs in the house and garden, and it can be used in various ways to improve cooking and even prevent culinary disasters. It keeps indefinitely and using it will save you lots of money as well as helping you avoid lots of dangerous chemicals in the home.

For thousands of years vinegar was used in many ways around the home, until the nineteenth century when branded (and often expensive and chemical-laden) products began to replace traditional natural remedies.

In summary, this cheap, natural and versatile liquid can be used to:

- Improve health
- Improve food and cooking
- Make cleaning easier
- Save money
- Help the environment

What is vinegar?
Vinegar or *Vin Aigre* in French, literally means sour wine, and is produced in the same way that wine is made, but with a higher concentration of something called acetic acid, which gives vinegar its sharp taste. This is then distilled into a clear spirit.

What type should I use?
The vinegar referred to in this book is white vinegar (a clear liquid), also called spirit or distilled vinegar, which has an acetic acid content of around 5-8%. In the UK a common and cheaper type of vinegar is malt vinegar, which is suitable for cooking and taking internally, but not for all cleaning jobs as it can leave brown stains.

A lot of websites and magazine articles, particularly American ones, refer to something called 'Apple Cider Vinegar', made from apples. It's often touted as a miracle cure for all kinds of ailments. There are theories that this is better for the health than other vinegars, but there is little conclusive evidence for this, and in terms of acetic acid content (the active ingredient) it's much the same as distilled vinegar.

'Pickling vinegar' usually contains spices, so is best avoided for cleaning jobs.

You may also see something called NBC or 'Non Brewed Condiment' which is an industrially produced vinegar substitute, used mainly by chip shops. This will do the same job as real vinegar for certain cleaning jobs, but is probably best avoided for taking internally except for a light sprinkling on chips, for which it is intended.

Some people prefer to use white vinegar for cleaning and external use on the body, and apple cider vinegar for taking internally due to its supposed greater health benefits, but white vinegar can be used for everything.

Won't everything smell of vinegar?
No. At first there will be a strong smell if undiluted vinegar is used for cleaning, etc, but this rapidly disperses, and in fact, vinegar is a strong deodoriser.

Tips to remember
The tips in this book are for guidance only and are used at your own risk. If you have a serious medical condition you should always consult a doctor before taking any natural remedies.

Remember that vinegar used for soaking things can be stored and reused many times. Keep it in a separate, clearly marked container so that you don't confuse this with clean vinegar.

The cheapest vinegar will work perfectly well. At time of writing, in the UK malt vinegar was available, for example, in Tesco for 99p for 2 litres, and white vinegar was 39p for 568ml.

Chinese supermarkets are a good source of cheap white vinegar.

A spray bottle is required for many tips in this book. These can be bought cheaply from pound shops (dollar stores) or you can reuse an old spray bottle if it is thoroughly cleaned and relabelled.

Measurements
You don't need to worry too much about getting amounts exactly right when trying the tips in this book, but the measurements shown roughly equate to metric as follows:

1 cup (US cup) is approximately 240 ml, slightly less than half a pint
1 teaspoon is approximately 5ml
1 dessert spoon is approximately 10ml
1 table spoon is approximately 15ml.
1 pint is approximately 568ml
1 gallon is approximately 4.5 litres

Vinegar uses

Acidity in soil, to increase: add 1 cup of vinegar to 1 gallon of tap water when watering plants.

Aftershave substitute: mix equal parts vinegar and water to sterilise cuts and close pores.

Age spots (liver spots), to remove: dab on neat vinegar with a cotton bud (Q tip) daily, or secure cotton wool soaked in vinegar over the area for 30 minutes each day until it is gone.

Air, to freshen: to remove smells from the air, spray neat vinegar lightly into the air.

Animals, to deter: animals such as cats, foxes, dogs etc can be kept out of gardens by soaking rags in neat vinegar and placing them at entry points.

Ants, to deter: spray neat vinegar in nests or where ants congregate.

Appetite, to reduce: drinking 1 teaspoon of vinegar in 1 cup of water is said to reduce appetite and help in dieting.

Arthritis, to relieve: 1 teaspoon of vinegar in 1 cup of water taken 3 times daily is said to reduce the symptoms of arthritis.

Athlete's foot, to treat: some types of athlete's foot are said to respond well to soaking in vinegar with a cloth every day.

Ball point pen ink, to remove: rub stain with neat vinegar.

Baths, to clean: spray neat vinegar then sprinkle bicarbonate of soda. Leave for a few minutes then rinse.

Bicycle chains, to degrease: spray on neat vinegar or remove and soak in vinegar overnight. Works for most grease-clogged machine parts.

Bird droppings, to remove: hardened bird droppings can be removed by spraying with neat vinegar. Leave for 20 minutes or so then rub off.

Body odour, to neutralise: vinegar can work as a cheap and natural deodorant, just spray on armpits and allow to dry.

Body odour, to remove from clothing: as a last resort, sometimes body odour can be removed from clothing by spraying on neat vinegar and allowing it to air dry.

Brass, to polish: dissolve 1 teaspoon of salt in 1 cup of vinegar and stir in flour to make a paste. Rub on and leave for 20 minutes, then rinse with water and rub clean.

Bread crusts, to improve: when baking bread, pies etc brush the pastry with vinegar a few minutes before removing from the oven.

Breath, to freshen: rinse mouth with equal parts water and vinegar.

Bricks, to clean: wipe with solution of 1 cup vinegar to 1 gallon of warm water.

Bruises, to reduce: applying vinegar to bruising is said to reduce swelling and discolouration.

Burnt-on food, to remove from pans: add equal parts vinegar and water to pan and bring to boil. Remove from heat and add 1 teaspoon baking soda. Leave to cool then clean as normal.

Buttermilk subsitute: mix 1 tablespoon of vinegar with 1 cup of milk; stand for 5 minutes then use as recipe requires.

Cane furniture, to revive: sagging cane furniture can be revived by sponging with equal parts vinegar and water. Leave in the sun or a warm room to dry.

Carpets, to remove stains from: mix 1 tsp liquid soap or detergent and 1 tsp of vinegar with 1 pint of water. Rub in gently with a cloth then rinse with clean water.

Cheese, to preserve: wrap in a cloth soaked in neat vinegar then place in the fridge or an airtight container.

Chewing gum, to remove from clothing or hair: heat neat vinegar in microwave and apply to gum, then remove gently.

Chopping boards, to clean and disinfect: scrub with neat vinegar.

Clothing, to whiten: boil white socks, underwear etc in a solution of 1 cup of vinegar to 3 pints of water. Turn off heat and soak overnight, then wash as normal.

Coffee makers, to clean: pour 2 cups of vinegar and 1 cup of water into the machine and run a full cycle; rinse with 2 cycles of fresh water.

Colour runs, to lessen: to minimise colour runs with new clothing, soak items in equal parts water and vinegar before washing.

Concrete stains, to treat: hands soiled with concrete, cement or other alkaline stains should be rubbed with neat vinegar before washing to help neutralise harmful chemicals.

Constipation, to relieve: 1 teaspoon taken in 1 cup of water twice daily is said to relieve constipation.

Corns and callouses, to remove: tape a piece of cloth or tissue soaked in vinegar to the affected area, and leave on overnight.

Crayon, to remove: rub stain with a toothbrush dipped in neat vinegar, then wipe off with a damp cloth.

Cuts, minor, to disinfect: wash with a solution of 1 tablespoon of vinegar to 1 pint of water.

Dandruff, to treat: after shampooing, rinse with a solutio of 1/2 cup vinegar to 2 cups water.

Dandruff, to treat: massage a solution of equal parts vinegar and water into the scalp, then shampoo as normal.

Dentures, to clean: soak overnight in equal parts water and vinegar, then clean as normal.

Deodorant stains, to remove: dab with neat vinegar and wash as normal.

Diabetes, to alleviate: 2 tablespoons of vinegar before meals is said by some sufferers to help alleviate diabetes.

Dogs, to deodorise: rub down with a mixture of 1 cup of vinegar to 2 gallons of water. Rub dry without rinsing.

Drains, to deodorise: pour 1 cup of vinegar down the drain, leave for 20 minutes then flush with cold water.

Dry skin, to relieve: add 2 tablespoons of vinegar to bath water.

Dry skin, to soften: soak cotton wool in neat vinegar and rub on, then rinse with clean water.

DVDs/CDs, to clean: polish with a very soft cloth and a small amount of neat vinegar.

Egg whites, to improve: spray neat vinegar lightly onto mixing bowls and beaters then wipe dry before beating eggs.

Eggs, to colour: to colour eggs at Easter, mix 1/2 teaspoon of vinegar with 1 cup of hot water, then add food colouring.

Eggs, to minimise leaking: if a crack appears while boiling, add 1 teaspoon of vinegar to the water to reduce leakage.

Eggs, to substitute: 1 tablespoon of vinegar mixed with 1 teaspoon of baking soda can be substituted for an egg in cake recipes.

Energy levels, to improve: a teaspoon of vinegar in a cup of water is said to improve energy levels, especially when exercising.

Fabrics, to soften: add 1 cup of vinegar to the washing machine rinse cycle.

Fish, to cook: soak in equal parts water and vinegar before cooking to improve flavour.

Fish, to prevent crumbling: add 1 tablespoon of vinegar to the water when boiling or poaching fish.

Fish, to scale: rub fish with vinegar then leave to soak for a few minutes to make scaling easier.

Flatulence, to reduce: adding a teaspoon of vinegar to the water that beans and vegetables are cooked in is said to reduce flatulence.

Fleas, to deter from pets: add 1/2 a teaspoon of vinegar per pint of drinking water.

Flies, to deter: fill a bowl with 2 pints of water, 2 tablespoons of sugar, 2 tablespoons of vinegar and a few drops of liquid soap. Flies which land in the mixture will be unable to escape.

Floors, to wash: add 1/2 cup of vinegar to a half gallon of warm water.

Flowers, to keep longer: add 1 tablespoon of sugar and 1 of vinegar to every pint of water in flower vases.

Foot odour, to treat: Mix 1 cup of vinegar with 2 gallons of warm water. Soak feet for 45 minutes regularly.

Fridges, to clean: wash with a solution of equal parts water and vinegar.

Fridges, to deodorise: place 1 cup of vinegar in the fridge and leave there until smells have gone.

Frost, to prevent on windscreens: spray with 3 parts vinegar to 1 part water the night before.

Fruit stains, to remove from skin: rub hands with neat vinegar.

Glasses, to clean in dishwasher: put 1 cup of vinegar in the bottom of the dishwasher before using as normal.

Grass, to kill: spray with neat vinegar.

Grease, to remove: wipe down greasy counters, tabletops etc with a solution of equal parts vinegar and warm water.

Greasy taste, to reduce: clean the inside of deep fat fryers with neat vinegar to reduce greasiness in food.

Grout, to clean: scrub with an old toothbrush soaked in neat vinegar.

Hair lice/nits, to kill: spray neat vinegar on the scalp and comb through, then rinse with clean water.

Hair, to improve shine: spray with neat vinegar, comb through then rinse with fresh water.

Hair, to untangle: spraying hair with vinegar then rinsing is said to reduce tangling.

Hay fever, to relieve: 2 teaspoons of vinegar in 1 cup of water taken 2-3 times a day is said to relieve hayfever.

Hiccups, to cure: swallowing a teaspoon of neat vinegar is said to cure hiccups.

Holes in cloth, to remove: holes left after removing hems or seams can be made less visible by placing a cloth moistened with neat vinegar under the fabric, then ironing.

Indigestion, to relieve: drink 1 teaspoon of vinegar in 1 cup of water.

Ink, to make: Strain 1/2 cup blackberries or similar into a cup and add 1/2 teaspoon of vinegar and 1/2 teaspoon salt. Mix well and dilute if required.

Insects, to repel: spraying vinegar on the skin is said to act as an insect repellent.

Irons, to clean: the sole plate of an iron can be cleaned with a mixture of 1 part vinegar and 1 part salt.

Irons, to unclog: steam irons can be cleaned by adding equal parts of water and vinegar to the tank. Turn on to steam setting and leave iron upright for 5 minutes, then turn off and allow to cool; empty tank and rinse with clean water.

Jar lids, to loosen: place jar upside down in neat vinegar for a few minutes.

Jars, to remove residue: to use up the last bits of sauce, dressing etc from jars and bottles, add a small amount of vinegar and shake well, then pour out.

Jeans, to prevent fading: soak in bucket of cold water with 1 cup vinegar overnight before washing to prevent fading.

Jewellery, to clean: Soak in neat vinegar for 15 minutes, remove and dry with cloth.

Kettles, to clean: remove limescale from the inside of kettles by boiling 3 cups of neat vinegar. Leave to soak overnight then rinse with fresh water.

Kitchen smells, to remove: simmer equal parts of vinegar and water in a saucepan until smells have gone.

Laundry, to improve: add one cup of vinegar to the rinse cycle.
Lawnmower blades, to clean: to remove encrusted grass etc, wipe down with neat vinegar.

Leather, to revive: Mix equal parts vinegar and linseed oil and work in with a soft cloth, then rub off with clean cloth.

Lemon juice substitute: use neat vinegar in place of lemon juice when required in small amounts in recipes.

Meat, to tenderise: soak in a mixture of 1 cup vinegar to 2 cups water (or oil and water) and stand for 2 hours.

Meringues, to improve: add 1 teaspoon of vinegar for every 3 or 4 eggs used.

Microwaves, to clean: boil a solution of 1/4 cup vinegar and 1 cup of water. Wipe down surfaces when cool.

Mildew, to remove: if walls or woodwork are stained with mildew, spray with neat vinegar and wipe down with a clean cloth.

Nail polish, to improve: before painting, clean nails with cotton wool soaked in neat vinegar, to help varnish to adhere.

Nappies (diapers), to soak: if you use cloth nappies, add 1 cup of vinegar per 2 gallons of water in the nappy bucket to neutralise urine.

Nausea, to relieve: drink 1 cup of water mixed with 1 teaspoon of vinegar.

Olives, to preserve: fresh olives can be made to last longer by keeping them submerged in vinegar.

Onion smells, to remove: rub neat vinegar on hands before and after chopping onions.

Ovens, to clean: spray with neat vinegar and sprinkle on baking soda. Leave to fizz for a while then wipe off.

Paint, to improve: spraying neat vinegar on surfaces such as cement or galvanised steel before painting (allow vinegar to dry first) is said to improve adhesion.

Paintbrushes, to soften: soak in hot vinegar then clean with soapy water.

Painted walls and woodwork, to clean: mix 1 cup ammonia, 1/2 cup vinegar and 1/4 cup baking soda with 1 gallon of warm water. Wipe down with soft cloth and rinse with clear water.

Pecking chickens, to prevent: adding 1 tablespoon of vinegar to 1 gallon of chickens' drinking water is said to make them less likely to peck one another.

Piano keys, to clean: wipe down with mixture of 1/2 cup vinegar to 2 cups water.

Pie crusts, to improve: add 1 teaspoon of vinegar to the mixture.

Piles (haemorrhoids), to relieve: dabbing equal parts vinegar and water on piles is said to give relief in some cases.

Plaster, to improve: add 1/2 teaspoon of vinegar to 1 pint of plaster to give a longer working time.

Polish, to remove: to remove build up of wax polish on furniture, wipe down with solution of equal parts vinegar and water, then dry with clean cloth.

Potatoes, to whiten: 1 teaspoon of vinegar added to the water in which potatoes are boiling will keep them white.

Rice, to avoid stickiness: add 1 teaspoon of vinegar to the water when boiling.

Rice, to prevent sticking: add 1 teaspoon of water to every 2 cups of water when boiling rice, to help prevent sticking.

Rings, to remove from wood: mix equal parts vinegar and olive oil and rub in with a soft cloth.

Rugs, to revive: clean with brush or broom soaked in solution of 1 cup vinegar to 1 gallon of water.

Rust stains, to remove from clothing: rub gently with equal parts vinegar and hot water.

Rust, to remove: soak bolts, screws etc overnight in neat vinegar to remove rust.

Salad dressing: a frugal salad dressing can be made by mixing 3 tablespoons of olive oil with 2 tablespoons of vinegar, plus a pinch of salt and mixed herbs.

Salt stains, to remove from shoes: mix equal parts water and vinegar and dab on the stains until cleared.

Salty meat, to neutralise: mix 1 teaspoon of vinegar and 1 teaspoon of salt in with the water when boiling salty meat such as ham.

Sanitiser, multi-purpose: for a general sanitising spray for surfaces etc mix equal parts vinegar and water.

Scissors, to clean: spray with neat vinegar then clean with dry cloth.

Scorch marks, to remove from fabric: rub gently with a cloth soaked in neat vinegar, then wash as normal.

Scouring powder, to make: mix equal parts salt, vinegar and flour.

Shaving brushes, to soften: soak in equal parts vinegar and water overnight.

Shoes, to deodorise: spray the inside of the shoe with neat vinegar then stuff with newspaper; leave overnight.

Shower doors, to clean: spray with neat vinegar and wipe clean, or use a window cleaner's wiper.

Shower heads, to unclog: fill a small plastic bag with neat vinegar and tie it around the shower head so that it is totally immersed. Leave overnight to soak.

Silver, to clean: mix 1/2 cup vinegar and 2 tablespoons baking soda. Soak silver in mixture for 2-3 hours then rinse and dry with a clean cloth.

Skin, to tone: vinegar acts as an astringent skin toner. wash with a flannel soaked in 1 part vinegar to 4 parts water.

Soil, to test: add vinegar to 1/4 cup of dry soil. If it fizzes, the soil is alkaline.

Soot, to remove from fireplace doors: wash with equal parts water and vinegar. Stubborn stains may be removed by soaking sheets of newspaper in vinegar and sticking them to the door overnight.

Sore muscles, to treat: holding a cloth or tissue soaked in vinegar to sore muscles, strains etc is said to relieve symptoms.

Sore throats, to treat: Gargle with a mixture of 1 cup water and 1 teaspoon of vinegar.

Soups, to improve flavour: add 1 teaspoon of vinegar to the soup while cooking.

Spectacles, to clean: put 1 small drop of vinegar on each lens and rub with a clean soft cloth.

Sponges and loofahs, to revive: soak in equal parts vinegar and water for 24 hours, then rinse with fresh water.

Sponges and rags, to clean: soak dishclothes, sponges etc regularly in neat vinegar overnight to clean them.

Stainless steel, to polish: spray vinegar onto a soft cloth and rub in until clean.

Sticker residue, to remove: spray with neat vinegar and wipe with a cloth until removed.

Stings, to sooth: spray neat vinegar on the affected area.

Suede shoes, to clean: wipe with a cloth soaked in equal parts vinegar and water.

Sunburn, to treat: mild cases of sunburn may be soothed by spraying with equal parts vinegar and water.

Sweat stains, to remove from clothing: scrub with paste made from 2 parts white vinegar to 3 parts baking soda. Leave for 30 minutes then wash as normal.

Sweetness, to remove: wine or fruit juice which tastes too sweet can be neutralised by adding a little vinegar.

Taps, to remove limescale from: soak tissues or kitchen roll in neat vinegar and press on to the affected areas. Leave overnight, then remove the paper and rub down with a damp cloth.

Teeth, to whiten: rinse with a solution of 1 tablespoon vinegar to 1 cup of water regularly, then rinse with fresh water.

Tobacco smells, to remove: if a room smells of tobacco smoke, place a bowl of neat vinegar in the area where the smell is strongest.

Toenail fungus, to treat: soak toes in solution of 1 part vinegar to 2 parts water for 15 minutes a day.

Toilets and sinks, to unblock. Pour 1 cup of baking soda and 2 cups of vinegar into the toilet or down the plughole, leave for 30 minutes then flush through. Repeat as required.

Toilets, to clean: pour 2 cups of neat vinegar into the bowl, leave overnight and then flush. Done regularly, this will minimise stains in the bowl.

Tonic: 1 teaspoon of vinegar to 1 cup of water taken daily is said to act as a general tonic.

Toothbrushes, to sanitise: spray with neat vinegar, leave overnight then rinse with clean water.

Urine smells, to remove from carpets: spray on neat, then rub with clean damp cloth. Test an inconspicuous area first.

Varicose veins, to reduce: rubbing neat vinegar on varicose veins every day is said to reduce them.

Vegetables, to freshen: revive wilted vegetables by soaking for 20 minutes in cold water with approx 1 dessert spoon of vinegar per pint.

Venetian blinds, to clean: soak cloth in equal parts vinegar and warm water, then wipe down. Dry with clean cloth.

Wallpaper, to remove: spray with neat vinegar and leave to soak for 30 minutes, then remove with scraper.

Warts, to remove: applying neat vinegar to warts daily may remove them.

Washing machines, to sanitise: add one cup of neat vinegar to the drum, then run machine empty for one cycle.

Washing up liquid (dish soap), to improve: add 2-3 tablespoons per litre of liquid, shake well and use as normal.

Water stains, to remove: glasses, vases etc with water stains can be treated by wiping or scrubbing neat vinegar on to the stain then rinsing with cold water. Leave vinegar on to soak for more stubborn stains.

Weeds, to kill: spray with neat vinegar. Beware, this will kill most plants, not just weeds, and will prevent regrowth in soil, so it is best used on patios, pavements etc.

Windows and mirrors, to clean: mix equal parts of vinegar and water and spray or wipe on. Dry with soft cloth.

Windscreen wipers, to clean: rub down with neat vinegar. Also works with household window cleaner wipers.

Woollens, to stretch: shrunken wool clothing can sometimes be brought back to its former shape by boiling in a solution of 1 part vinegar to 2 parts water for 25 minutes.

Wrinkles, to remove from clothing: spray with solution of 1 part vinegar to 3 parts water, then hang to dry.

Other titles from Montpelier Publishing

Available from Amazon

Frugal living

A Treasury of Thrift
Frontier Frugal
1001 Ways to Save Money
The Frugal Gentleman
The Men's Guide to Frugal Grooming
Garden Tips

Body, mind and spirit

Non-Religious Wedding Readings
The Simple Living Companion
How to be Happy
Non-Religious Funeral Readings
Spiritual Readings for Funerals
Marriage Advice: Dos and Don'ts for Husbands and Wives

Printed in Great Britain
by Amazon